Let's fly into this book ...

First Published 2025 by Jenny Dyer
For further information
contact through facebook page

Walking with Wildlife

or website

www.walkingwithwildlife.com.au

Text: © Jennifer Dyer 2025
Photography: © Jennifer Dyer 2024

All rights reserved. No part of this publication may be reproduced, stored in a retrieval system, or transmitted in any form or by any means electronic or mechanical, or by photocopying or otherwise without prior written permission of the author or copyright holder.

ISBN 978-1-7637939-7-2

Cover and Artwork: Jenny Dyer

Walking with Wildlife ™

BOOK 5 - SPRING TIME

Written by Jenny Dyer

Photography and Design by Jenny Dyer

This magpie was in the yard early this morning … looking for breakfast.

He managed to find a grub in the grass. Can you see it?

As I was having my early morning cup of tea, I heard more visitors. This beautiful male king parrot came to visit. He flew from one spot to the next, not worried about being close to me. They are very inquisitive, friendly birds.

A female king parrot even flew onto a little table on my patio. She was so close.

You shouldn't feed these birds as it reduces their ability to find food on their own in the wild.

That was a nice early morning surprise with one of my favourite birds!

It's that time again …. Let's go walking with wildlife.

As usual, I looked up into the gum trees, looking for any birds hiding in the branches and then I spied this Pacific Baza - one I had never seen before. There are so many different types of birds you will see when you look. Have you spotted any birds in the wild?

The Pacific Baza is also known as the Crested Hawk.

It's always nice to find a koala up in those gum trees but it's time for a peaceful sleep. Koalas are nocturnal animals and need their rest during the day.

I captured this photo of a brown cuckoo dove in the big gully. When he flew off, I watched which way he went and decided to back track and stalk him. He landed in a thick, dark scrub tree. I moved in very slowly and quietly, trying to hide from him as well. I thought he would fly away, but no, he was still in the tree.

He was just sitting up there all fluffed up.

As I was watching him he moved in the tree so I had to find him again.

He had moved closer to his mate. I didn't know there was another bird in there. The tree had very thick foliage and it was difficult to spot them as it was so dark, almost too dark for photos.

I later found there was a whole family of these birds. I'll have to keep my eye out for them. Hopefully I get to see them again.

As I walked further up the track I could hear the tawny grassbird's call but I couldn't see him. I stood still and tried to locate the direction of his call. I took a few quiet steps closer to him. Yes! He had something in his mouth.

He kept moving frantically from one spot to the next but he wasn't swallowing that grasshopper in his mouth.

Yet another move behind some twigs but he's not letting go of that grasshopper and he's not eating it either.

He was having trouble balancing on the stalk with the wind blowing hard. Just then I heard a screech going over the top of me. I looked up and it was …

… a brown falcon. He flew up into a tall tree. He sat there for a while then took a dive down into the grass.

He flew back up onto a branch with what looked like a fairy wren. He devoured it, pulling it apart bit by bit. Nature can be cruel sometimes.

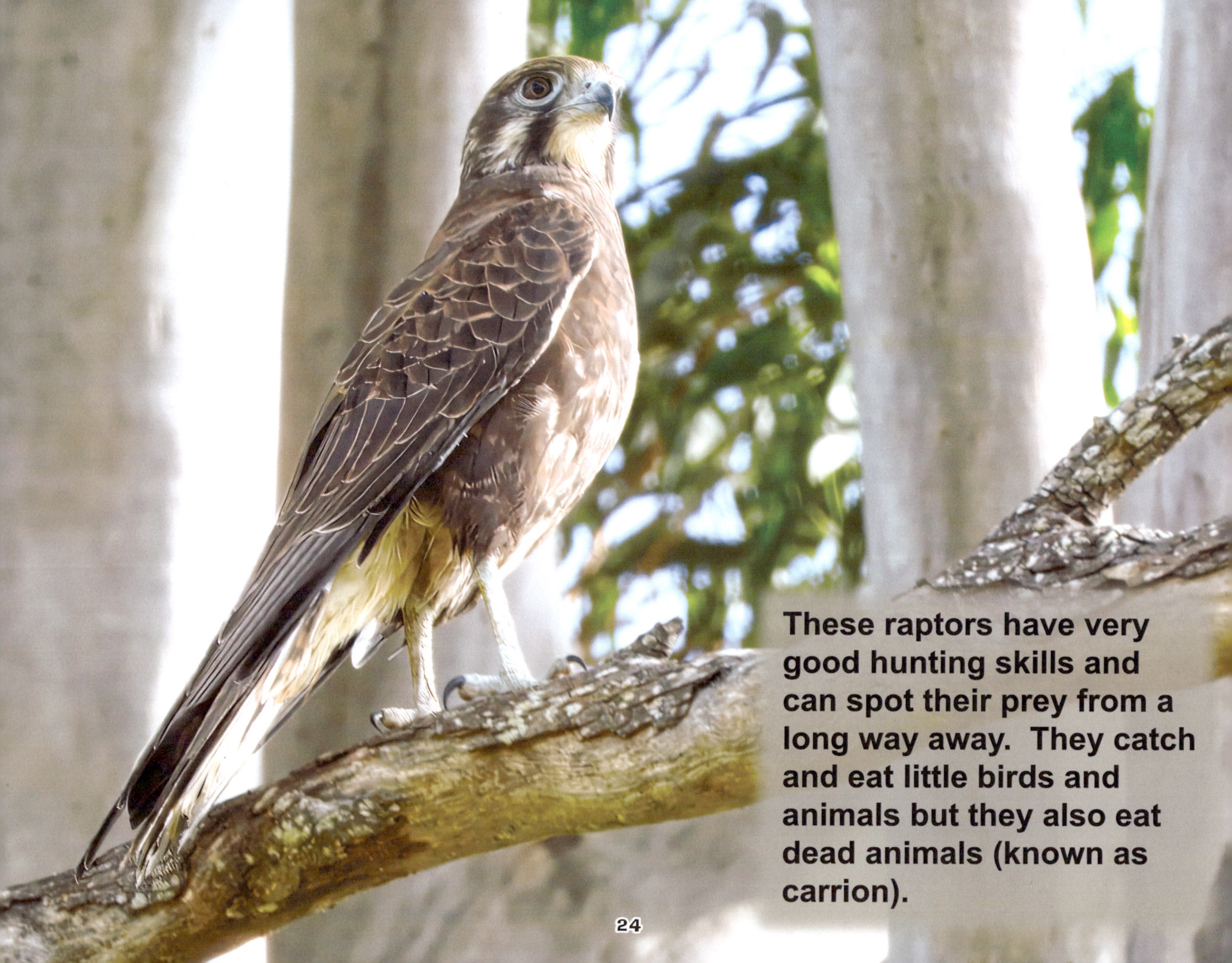

These raptors have very good hunting skills and can spot their prey from a long way away. They catch and eat little birds and animals but they also eat dead animals (known as carrion).

I often see this brown falcon sitting in this dead tree just waiting for something nice to eat.

As I walked further up the road I could hear the magpies harmonising.

Preening is another favourite activity at this hour of the morning.

We neared our neighbours' place and called in for a visit. Their beautiful grevillea tree was flowering and attracting the birds. The noisy miners were enjoying the blooms.

The rainbow lorikeets were also having a lovely time with the flowers. What a way to attract birds to your garden … plant native flowering trees.

Even the blue-faced honeyeaters were enjoying the flowers. You wouldn't think one tree could attract so many birds.

A little friarbird was sitting in the bottle brush tree nearby. Flowers provide food for insects too which also attracts different birds.

The little friarbird is a prehistoric looking bird. As well as feeding on the nectar and blossoms, they also eat insects, fruit and seeds. They tend to spend their time in trees and not on the ground.

As we walked up the hill into open grass country, we saw the pipits running up the track in front of us. They kept a safe distance from us by flying a few metres, landing, walking along for a while, then flying another few metres so we couldn't get too close.

Eventually they flew off onto a post for safety, where they could keep a better eye on us.

They feed on a variety of insects that they find in the grass.

When we reached the orchard, we found the rainbow lorikeets having a feed of bananas in the small plantation.

They are the most common bird in Australia. Wherever there are native flowers or fruit trees, they are there enjoying a feast.

Imagine what these birds would do to a banana plantation or orchard. They often just nip the fruit off and leave it to rot on the ground. Farmers do have a lot to contend with to get food to your table. They will use special bird netting to keep the birds from eating your food.

45

The rainbow lorikeets also love peaches. The big seeds of the peach, however, are poisonous as they contain cyanide.

Then I got the call from my grandson. He said:

"There was a snake in the chook pen eating our chickens. We caught it and we are going to let it go near the dam. Do you want to come and photograph it?"

I replied: "Of course, I'll be there soon".

These carpet pythons wrap themselves around their prey and strangle them. Then they swallow their captives whole.

We let this python go well away from the chook pen where he won't take the chickens again.

Once we let him go, he quickly climbed up through the undergrowth into the tree. He then stopped to have a look at me.

Luckily I have a long zoom lens and didn't have to get close as he was in a strike position.

Then he headed to the top of the tree out of harm's way and I headed back home, my walk with wildlife over for another day.

What an amazing day it was! Thank you for joining me. I'll see you next time.

Can you name these birds and animals?

- Carpet Python
- King Parrot
- Magpie
- Noisy Miner
- Blue-Faced Honeyeater
- Pacific Baza
- Rainbow Lorikeet
- Koala
- Brown Falcon
- Tawny Grassbird
- Pipit
- Brown Cuckoo Dove
- Little Friarbird

Can you guess what type of bird this is?

Please join my Facebook page …

Walking with Wildlife

www.ingramcontent.com/pod-product-compliance
Lightning Source LLC
Chambersburg PA
CBRC101355070526
44583CB00010B/195